# Rhymes for Every Reason and Season

*A Journey Through Life's Moments*

LYNN D. GOBERT

# Rhymes for Every Reason and Season

Rhymes for Every Reason and Season

© 2024 by Lynn Gobert

All rights reserved. No part of this publication may be reproduced, distributed, or transmitted, in any form or by any means, including photocopying, recording, or other electronic or mechanical methods, without prior written permission of the publisher, except in the case of brief quotations, embodied in critical reviews and certain other noncommercial uses permitted by copyright law.

ISBN 978-1-7375713-5-3

Library of Congress Cataloging -in- Publication Data applied for

Editor: Cultivate Press

Womack House Publishing, LLC.
3965 East Brookstown Drive
Baton Rouge, LA 70805
225-356-1446
info@womackhouse.com

We hope you enjoy this book from Womack House Publishing. Our mission is to create works that inspire, uplift, and connect with readers around the world. To learn more about the author and explore other titles, visit www.womackhouse.com.

For Bulk Ordering and Press Inquiries

Womack House Publishing, LLC.

225-356-1446

info@womackhouse.com

Printed in the United States of America

# Dedication

This book is dedicated to all those that I love and who love me. Their enthusiasm and encouragement provided the energy that propelled me to prepare these pieces to be shared and hopefully enjoyed by others. My deepest regret is that my most supportive fan and sister, Ruth is no longer here, in the natural, to see this giant step.

# Table of Contents

**DEDICATION** ............................................................................. **III**

**INTRODUCTION** ....................................................................... **VI**

1. A Smile ............................................................................. 1
2. A Life Well-Spent ............................................................. 4
3. Answered Prayer .............................................................. 7
4. Decisions ........................................................................ 10
5. Encouragement .............................................................. 13
6. Fear ................................................................................ 16
7. Forgiveness .................................................................... 19
8. Light ............................................................................... 22
9. Living Holy ..................................................................... 25
10. Peace in Darkness ......................................................... 28
11. Power and Grace ........................................................... 31
12. Right or Righteous ........................................................ 34
13. Self-Control ................................................................... 37
14. Something is Going to Happen ..................................... 40
15. Struggle ......................................................................... 43
16. My Best .......................................................................... 46
17. The Life Road ................................................................ 48
18. The Meek ....................................................................... 51
19. The Message ................................................................. 54
20. The Rescue .................................................................... 57
21. The Toolbox ................................................................... 60
22. Waiting .......................................................................... 63
23. What Works ................................................................... 65

| 24. | Am I Sure It's You | 68 |
| --- | --- | --- |
| 25. | Growth | 71 |
| 26. | Disappointments | 74 |
| 27. | Willful Blindness | 77 |
| 28. | GRIEF | 80 |
| 29. | A Family | 83 |
| 30. | Am I a Solider | 86 |
| 31. | Love and Victory | 89 |
| 32. | The Message | 92 |
| 33. | Where Did They Go | 95 |
| 34. | WHY? | 98 |
| 35. | Who Are You | 101 |
| 36. | Your Song | 104 |
| 37. | Ordinary | 106 |
| 38. | Confidence or Arrogance | 109 |
| 39. | Dim or Dazzle | 112 |
| 40. | Miss Lollygag | 115 |
| 41. | Mr. Man | 118 |
| 42. | Something Precious | 121 |
| 43. | Blame and Shame | 124 |

# Rhymes for Every Reason and Season

# Introduction

An evolution would be the best way to describe how this book came to be. I first began authoring short poems about my siblings and our early childhood years. I intended to read them at future family gatherings. I thought they would be funny and create a unique addition to family holiday traditions. Furthermore, I hoped they would help to preserve our rich upbringing for the younger members of the family.

As time went on, I found it comforting to write about current events of my life and the lives of others in my orbit. My poems brought me a sense of achievement, closure, and even satisfaction. Even though, at the time it was not my goal to ever publish any of them. I viewed my writing as a vehicle used to freely voice my opinions, release my frustrations, and air my strong beliefs. Drafting poems has come to be one of my greatest "stress relievers."

My body of work encompasses day-to-day challenges in the lives of many. I passionately believe, by processing my thoughts, it offered a clearer picture and thereby resulted in a wiser decision. Finally, I thought that sharing my work could encourage others in the same way they comforted me. I sincerely hope my poems will serve to foster useful and uplifting purposes.

# 01

# A Smile

A smile is a simple facial expression.
Humans and some animals do it naturally, without practice or persuasion.
However, a smile has such great and lasting effects.
It can change life decisions – simple or complex.

A sincere smile welcomes honest conversation.
A gentle one softens the blow of disturbing information.
It forecasts pure motives understood in any culture.
And captures the inner beauty of a kind gesture.

Wearing a smile when entering a new venue or space.
Gives an illusion of confidence, even though that may not be the case.
A smile is a useful communication tool.
That does not require knowledge of etiquette or social rules.

# Rhymes for Every Reason and Season

A smile carries words farther than speech alone.
Because it can penetrate a heart made of the most solid stone.
A genuine smile is inexpensive but has high sustainable worth.
Able to extend hope and good cheer throughout the entire earth.

*A Journey Through Life's Moments*

# Reflections

# A Life Well-Spent

Childhood is filled with learning through teaching and mischief.
Slowly we gain independence from experiences and belief.
We make friends and acquaintances who are like us in many ways.
The bond we share may last a lifetime or just a few days.

In our teens, we believe we have it all figured out.
But we soon face challenges that prove we had no clue what life was all about.
We thank God for parents or mentors who came to the rescue.
They showed us the wiser and less costly point of view.

We mature, we meet and marry that special someone.
Our Prince or Queen who lights up our days like the beauty of the morning sun.
As the years pass, children grow, and circumstances occur.

It may be hard to remember how sweet those former days were.

Life goes on; situations and problems distract and hold your attention.

By now we have learned to lean on each other and God, trusting he will complete the mission.

Finally, old age has its role to play.

It is at this point wisdom has come to stay.

We know what is good and worth doing.

So, we rely on God's guidance instead of aimlessly wandering.

We see we have been blessed by wondrous and powerful life events.

And more than anything else, **we have lived a life that was well-spent**.

# Reflections

*A Journey Through Life's Moments*

# Answered Prayer

Praying to God is a divine mandate.
It is having conversation with the Most Holy – the graciously Great.
As conversations go, it is communication from one to another.
Both contributing and exchanging dialogue for future application to discover.

There is expectation that comes with prayer.
That the request will be managed with loving-compassionate care.
It is with Faith that the process begins.
It would be a waste of valuable time if we did not anticipate results in the end.

But are we really praying or telling?
Are we spewing out orders and demands to God who is All Mighty and All Knowing?
Yes, He told us to always pray and never cease.
But He knows what is best and what are our true needs.

# Rhymes for Every Reason and Season

The greatest problem we encounter with the answering of prayer.

Is accepting the fact – the timing of the answer is God's to declare.

Our answer may come in three diverse ways.

It may be yes, no, or wait for many, many.

days.

*A Journey Through Life's Moments*

# Reflections

# Decisions

Making decisions is an all-day, everyday function.
We decide what to eat, what to wear, and where to go almost by a reflex action.
But many other decisions require much more in-depth thought.
In order to reach the positive outcome that is sought.

A good decision must be based on firm and factual information.
And understanding the current circumstances and future ramifications.
Consideration should be given to all that the change will impact.
Haste should not replace careful evaluation of supporting facts.

Clear and unselfish thinking will promote a fair solution.
Permitting others input assists with the final conclusion.
Allowing the presence of opposite points of view.
Is a sign of honorable intentions that are long overdue.

There is a sense of satisfaction that comes when a decision is made.

Especially, when all concerns were equally displayed.

When YES is the answer to the final question posed to the many or few:

Is it useful, is it fair, and is it true?

# Reflections

*A Journey Through Life's Moments*

# Encouragement

There is a need deeply embedded in each soul.
A yearning to complete a task or reach a goal.
Once the project is fully achieved.
A sense of accomplishment is joined to a sigh of relief.

Sooner than later another opportunity comes to produce or create.
Again, the challengers arrive- What, When and How, engage with their debate.
These carry with them fear of failure and stress.
All working together to hinder forward progress.

Continuing with a persistent, deliberate, and purposeful motion.
Requires discipline and unwavering devotion.
Diligence and dedication are extremely helpful ingredients, too.
When added to this mixture, they attract others to view.

# Rhymes for Every Reason and Season

People take notice of determined efforts to succeed.

Onlookers see demanding work as a prelude to a place of honor guaranteed.

Many will also offer words of encouragement and cheers of support.

Encouraging words are among the greatest elements our mind can import.

No matter how many times we do a task well.

Regardless of how many areas of skills and talents in which we may excel.

We all want to hear someone say," job well done."

Or get a supportive nudge that inspires us onward to run.

*A Journey Through Life's Moments*

# Reflections

# Fear

Fear is an unfaithful friend.
A predictor of a tragic end.
A robber of abundant living.
Constantly at odds with generosity and giving.

It is a distracting cloud of regret and despair.
Blocking our view of hope with darkness in the air.
Fear wishes we don't take notice of the moon or the stars.
That are just a short distance – not too far.

Fear is a bully that pretends to possess extreme power.
Its strength is ours that we release when we cower.
Fear wants to stop our forward progress.
Believing we'll never embrace a heart for ultimate success.

Thank God for giving Fear a worthy opponent.

That stands firm and is solidly dominant.

Fear will always be defeated by Faith.

Because Faith believes and shouts "victory" while the battle is yet taking place.

# Reflections

*A Journey Through Life's Moments*

# 07

# Forgiveness

We hear the familiar phrase, "It's hard to forgive," almost every day.

People then describe the hurt and pain that seems never to go away.

The expectation appears to be that the act of forgiving involves loss of memory.

And the process is not complete unless all is forgotten or at least blurry.

Hurt feelings, evil deeds, and anger are not easy to forget!

Their sting lingers for days on end – never needing a recharge or reset.

We all possess human emotions that are fragile and tender.

Even the strongest person is vulnerable to emotional bruising from a crafty accuser.

# Rhymes for Every Reason and Season

But what part does forgiveness play in this delicate event?
Can anything good be gained by this unfortunate incident?
Will the victim forever be damaged by what was done?
Does forgiveness have benefits that allow the wounded to overcome?

Forgiveness is a "freedom-finding agent" with liberating power!
When the victim forgives, they are set free from unquenchable anger!
Their creativity again blossoms uninhibited, as it was meant to flow!
Stress no longer reigns free to fester and rapidly grow.

The benefits of forgiving by far outweigh.
hanging on to bad memories that cause feelings of dismay.
When forgiveness takes its final bow.
The curtain of despair closes-no more pain to allow.
Restoration and renewed power return once again.
Vowing never to permit cheerfulness and joy to rescind.

*A Journey Through Life's Moments*

# Reflections

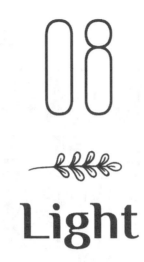

# Light

Illumination, brightness, and radiant
describe the properties that make light so brilliant.
Light shines automatically- as a matter of fact.
And does not require any motivation; it simply performs the act.

Light is a reliable source of energy and fuel.
It is a catalyst that is a vital igniting tool.
Without the presence of the richness of light
The full beauty of nature could not be captured by human eyesight.

Light, then causes the senses to awaken,
It cannot be unnoticed or unwittingly mistaken.
Its existence is felt even when it is not fully understood.
Light boldly demonstrates things that are honest and good.

We say we are the lights, and we do shine.

But we also say the world is dark and in moral decline.

What else can we do to change this awful predicament?

We pray for safety and a peaceful environment.

Maybe we should examine our little light more closely.

Are we holding it high enough for all to see it clearly?

Should we work harder to share our faith everywhere we go?

Showing kindness and concern in abundance to the point of overflow.

This is the time for recommitment and rededication.

A time to give full-force attention to a total humankind restoration.

A return to the core mission of our Christian belief.

To care for others with compassionate love and Godly-enthusiasm.

**Rhymes for Every Reason and Season**

# Reflections

*A Journey Through Life's Moments*

# Living Holy

Does living a Holy life cause someone to look a noteworthy way?
Does being Holy make a difference in the things we say?
Can what we eat and what we drink,
Cause changes in our mood and the way we think?

Should we quote scripture to everyone we meet?
Should our style of dress be simple, discreet or just neat?
Should our speech be slow and deliberate?
And our body movements measurably moderate?

Being Holy starts with a deep yearning to know God intimately.
To love Him and strive to obey Him completely.
Making Micah, sixth chapter and verse eight
A daily model to observe and integrate.

# Rhymes for Every Reason and Season

A life dedicated to spreading God's Love every way, in every day.

Providing guidance to those who have gone astray.

Always ready to lend a helping hand.

With a sympathetic ear to listen and understand.

A Holy life requires the application of Godly principles.

In every situation whether complex or simple.

Making an honest assessment of ourselves.

By acknowledging God's amazing grace as the reason and not anyone else.

*A Journey Through Life's Moments*

# Reflections

# 10

# Peace in Darkness

It may seem impossible to be at peace,

When where we are going, we cannot see.

In darkness, hope and joy are hidden.

Because darkness, in full control, has demanded the presence of light to be forbidden.

Darkness has accompanying associates and close friends.

A group that is inseparable to the very end.

Some of their names are Depression, Heartache, and Fear.

Together they can dominate and cause many tears.

There is another unlikely, unexpected element that walks with these knaves.

Without invitation, it arrives with the strength to alter or make waves.

Because of its nature, it is not combative – but yet confident.

Peace presence brings harmony that is clearly evident.

Darkness does not have to disappear when peace comes.

But it does have to surrender or unwillingly succumb.
When peace assumes its dual position.
It shows they can co-exist in any conflict or condition.

Because Peace flows like a sparkling river.
Calm, patience, and tranquility is what it gently delivers.
Even though its effects cannot always be explained.
Our soul responds to Peace in a joyful exclaim.

# Rhymes for Every Reason and Season

# Reflections

*A Journey Through Life's Moments*

# Power and Grace

Power is bold and unapologetic.
Power's position of confident control is simply automatic.
It does not shrink when opposition beats its drum.
Its nature is to hold firm – defeat never being an option to succumb.

A powerful person is not always rude.
Their authority commands respect but arrogance – it does not necessarily include.
The powerful can easily be corrupt if they stand alone.
Allowing no one to tell them if they are right or wrong.

Grace comes in many forms.
An extension of time or a refinement that is out of the norm.
Grace is as notable as Power.
Because both stand out like a rare-colored flower.

# Rhymes for Every Reason and Season

The combination of Power and Grace makes for a lovely pair.

Together they move mountains with strength and a majestic flair.

When they work together in complete rhythm.

The results are awe, praise, and hopeful optimism.

*A Journey Through Life's Moments*

# Reflections

# 12

# Right or Righteous

Did you notice the man on the left-side of the street?

He was wearing a heavy overcoat in 90-degree heat.

Why would he do something so odd and strange?

Is he trying to draw attention in hopes to make a pivot or life change?

Does he believe eventually someone will stop and inquire?

Is this a humble cry for help with a situation that is dark or dire?

Or is this just a ploy to take advantage of a caring soul?

A Christian who makes serving others their daily goal.

What's the lady's story holding the small cardboard sign.

That makes her vulnerable to tender compassion or a sharp decline.

Is she lazy and refuse to carry her own weight?

Or was her career abruptly ended due to an ill-advised debate.

What should we believe about the people we pass by?
Could they be God-Sent angels meant to cause a pause or a sigh?
Should we ponder whether to donate a dollar or two?
Or tell ourselves, "they're plotting to do harm to you"

The right response may be to look and then move on
After all, being late for church would cause our favored pew-spot to be gone.
Righteousness should force us to stop and render heartfelt care.
Angel or not, God told us to freely share.

Following the laws of the land makes us right.
Being socially moral affords us a badge that shines very bright.
But the crown that fits the absolute best
Is the crown of righteousness- the believers' divine quest.

# Reflections

# 13

# Self-Control

Having control of one's actions and reactions is a perpetual task.
It requires the ability to manage raw emotions with an unassuming mask.
Self-control separates potential impulses and sudden desires.
From a sound decision that will be of lasting benefit – not a brief pacifier.

Self-control is a fruit of the Spirit.
A fruit that is undeniably rigid.
Wherever it is presented or can be observed
It stands out like an oddly shaped curve.

There are many components working in rhythm with each other.
To create an environment of restraint with a calming aura.
It takes insight and foresight to name a few.
To pause before making a move that may not be easy to undo.

# Rhymes for Every Reason and Season

A person who demonstrates self-control is attractive to many.

Their demeanor is in direct contrast to the mundane and ordinary.

They assess a situation using logic and reflective reasoning.

Then take a measured approach that is productive and lasting.

*A Journey Through Life's Moments*

# Reflections

# 14

## Something is Going to Happen

Things become chaotic and outright strange.

In situations where the obvious resolution could easily be arranged.

A slight workable pivot in a productive course

Becomes a complete circle with a violent confrontational force.

When personal ambition and a self-centered goal,

cause the loss of integrity and seize all mental control.

When nothing matters but what matters to you.

Focus is present but only in a tunnel view.

If doing wrong feels like the logical thing to do.

Telling a lie or withholding what is honorable and true.

Using crafty tricks and schemes to get ahead.

Wreaking havoc on someone whose success you intensely dread.

These acts bring with them the direst of consequences.

Justice will not allow such madness to prevail or persist.

Time is the keeper of retribution and the return of mutual respect.

On a prescribed - predestined day, vengeance arrives to defend and correct.

Suddenly situations that seem impossible to make right.

The powerful who could never be defeated in a fight.

Will be rendered totally powerless and completely overtaken.

By foundational life principles that are fair and unshaken.

# Reflections

# 15

# Struggle

There is nothing about a struggle that invokes pleasure and anxious anticipation.

Most would rather pivot in a less complicated, more predictable direction.

Struggling requires a forceful and intentional resistance,

Against seemingly insurmountable odds-strong and persistent.

A struggle presents challenges far beyond what we have ever conceived.

Causing feelings of overwhelmingness and thoughts that success will not be achieved.

It has no practical concept of time.

Struggles arrive unexpectedly and linger much longer than a reasonable paradigm.

# Rhymes for Every Reason and Season

The struggle is a test from which we gain life-changing rewards.

Even though the process is very gruesome and extremely hard.

The test reveals, to us, our most powerful strengths, and weak attributes.

Producing useful tools to withstand future setbacks or disputes.

You may still ask, "what are the real rewards for going through a strenuous test?"

Added strength, endurance, and perseverance are the first notable conquest.

Then a greater depth of Godly-Wisdom and Faithfulness comes into our view.

Showing us that God is our source of strength -the supreme reward of incomparable value.

*A Journey Through Life's Moments*

# Reflections

# 16

# My Best

When I complete a task like a project or test
How can I be sure I have done my absolute best?
Do I truly know when I have given it my All?
There is nothing left to add and nothing to recall.

How does it feel when everything has been said and done?
The search for innovative ideas has produced none.
No additional signs or dreams have burst from inside.
No powerful revelations or confirmation can be applied.

The assurance that this is the best I have to display.
Comes in a mysterious and subtle way.
The signal of a job that is altogether complete.
Is comparable to a calm and gentle breeze, which brings a sweet, satisfying relief.

*A Journey Through Life's Moments*

# Reflections

# The Life Road

Life is an ever-unfolding mystery.
It daily reveals small pieces of what will become our history.
Life is filled with valleys and peaks,
that leaves memories of emptiness and joyous mystique.

Life is a journey that leads to the unknown.
A steady pace makes each step intentional and willfully strong.
Plans are made with meaningful goals in mind.
Even though there are no guarantees of achievement or a perfect pattern of design.

What challenges cause us to continue on the Life Road?
What energizes a person to walk onward without a map or direct code?
Why do our natural instincts urge us to stay in the fight?
While not having a clear path showing us our direction is right?

*A Journey Through Life's Moments*

We are blessed with the will and determination to succeed.

We were created for greatness – never to settle or concede.

We are not traveling on this Life Road alone.

We have the Supreme Tour Navigator, who guides from His Heavenly Throne.

# Reflections

*A Journey Through Life's Moments*

# 18

# The Meek

Meek is a trait that to some is a disguise.

The person appears to be naïve and severely unwise.

Their actions and reactions are interpreted as passive or even weak.

Especially when they do not respond with anger after a brutal defeat.

The meek are rare in this present time.

Where acts of loud outbursts and rudeness are at a steady climb.

People seem not to care about the harm they bring.

Or that at some point vengeance's solemn bell will surely ring.

Meekness is power that is under control.

Wisdom to know when to be silent and when to be bold.

Knowing what to say and how to say it.

Recognizing how to persist and when to quit.

# Rhymes for Every Reason and Season

Maybe meekness is somewhat deceiving to some.

It is mysterious in nature because of where it comes from.

It is keenly aware of what its reward is utterly worth.

Meekness bears in mind that God said they will inherit the earth.

*A Journey Through Life's Moments*

# Reflections

# 19

# The Message

I want my message to be loud and clear.
Leaving no room for misinterpretation or ill will.
My words and deeds agree with each other.
What I say and what I do – not to sway or waiver.

Consistency and patience show in my everyday affairs.
Not yielding to being judgmental and unwilling to share.
I desire to be a defender of moral justice.
But equally promoting mercy as my instinctive practice.

I pray to have a seat at the Wisdom Table.
Equipped to impart useful counsel that is just and stable.
My record reflects what I said and what I exhibited is right.
I did not compromise for the sake of being polite.

My desired message comes from a place of deep humility.
I know I cannot achieve it with my own human ability.
God is the giver of this noble message.
I look to Him to deliver this divine package.

# Reflections

*A Journey Through Life's Moments*

# The Rescue

We often hear of a valiant rescue.

Someone being saved from the hands of an evil crew.

The rescue is a victorious and joyful end.

A direct contrast to the pain and sadness that could have been.

Another kind of rescue comes to my mind.

One that does not get the attention it deserves from all of humankind.

This rescue is not known or accepted by ALL.

Yet it's built to last forever, never subject to repair or recall.

Rescue is not the word generally chosen to describe what was achieved on the Cross.

But our sins were captured forever, without mishap or loss.

The plan of salvation was perfect in design.

No details overlooked – each part precisely aligned.

# Rhymes for Every Reason and Season

Because His motive for the rescue was so plain and simple
Some find it hard to accept its straightforward principle.
Love and love alone was the only basis for our rescue.

**All Praise to Jesus for His uniquely Unmatched Virtue!**

*A Journey Through Life's Moments*

# Reflections

# 21

# The Toolbox

The spiritual toolbox is filled with the finest of tools.

Like prayer, forgiveness, and the Golden Rule.

The box itself is made of strong and lasting metal.

Structured on the Word of God which causes confusion to settle.

So, the next time I'm upset, feeling defeated and my mood is low.

I hope I make a wise choice of where I allow my emotions to go.

Allowing temporal matters to flood my space of calm.

Alters my focus from joy and contentment – my faithful healing balm.

Feelings of deep dejection and being utterly disrespected.

are common, everyday feelings that are not pleasant but can be expected.

There is no way to escape these uncomfortable events

They are but a part of the total human experience.

Maintaining inward peace and contentment
Is achieved from the use of the appropriate equipment.
A toolbox that is filled with righteousness, faith, and peace.
Will repair all brokenness – causing despair to cease.

# Rhymes for Every Reason and Season

# Reflections

*A Journey Through Life's Moments*

# 22

# Waiting

Wait means to remain in place.
Anticipating the next steps in a race.
It's not a time to give up or to quit.
Waiting is the point where we reflect and regain our grit.

It's an intricate part of a perfected task.
Looking like a stop but really, it's a broad contrast.
While in the waiting mode, planning and logistical preparation is at play.
Details are being shaped to prevent an unexpected delay.

Unlike its homonym, weight- a measure of body mass
Wait is the presence of a non-physical action while time passes.
A weight measurement can be seen in an instant.
The result of the wait is revealed when the project is brought into existence.

# Reflections

# What Works

I need to put into practice the words of wisdom I hear and read.

Becoming a doer; the one who humbly takes heed.

I will purposely study the Bible daily without fail.

Then allow the Holy Spirit's direction to prevail.

Repeating "catchy phrases" will not get me through life's distressing tests.

Knowing and believing in God's Holy Word is what works best.

Increasing my faith is the key to achieving perfect peace.

Obtaining Divine contentment creates the joy that I seek.

Relying on God to work things out,

is a much better plan than me trying to chart the route.

He already knows the right way to go.

And He is able and willing to navigate through valleys, no matter how low.

# Rhymes for Every Reason and Season

He told me to take everything to Him in prayer.
that all my burdens, He would freely share.
So why am I weighed down with loads so heavy?
When God said, all my struggles He would help me carry.

*A Journey Through Life's Moments*

# Reflections

## 24

## Am I Sure It's You

Is this the right time to move?
Is there nothing left to solve or prove?
Is this the end of a familiar course?
Or the beginning of a new path filled with mystery and perforce?

Where does fear and hesitation come from?
Are they but natural reactions, relatives of anticipation of what's to come?
Does complacency also play a part in this mode?
Could it be the cause of progress being stagnant or slowed?

Yet, there is a sense of urgency deep within.
To create, innovate, and allow freshness to begin.
Each time creativity sends a spark of light,
Feelings of completeness and fulfillment ignite.

The questions, however, still remain.
What do I do with all I have gained?
Are you taking me to parts unknown?
Is it your voice telling me to move on?

# Reflections

*A Journey Through Life's Moments*

# Growth

Fertile soil, water, sunlight, and seeds
Common minerals but invaluable to human existential needs.
All are necessary to produce the intended result.
No substitute or variation will reap the harvest that is sought.

Absent of time and nourishment, no evolution will take place.
A resolute cultivator must bring intensive care at a steady pace.
The caring cultivator and time are also essential elements.
Needed to bring forth a healthy crop worthy of procurement.

Personal development requires basic but reliable components as well.
Knowledge, wisdom, and then application is vital to excel.
Securing these elements is a process involving outside resources.
And a receptive mind, eager to embrace new paths and unfamiliar courses.

# Rhymes for Every Reason and Season

Useful information is at the foundation of societal enrichment and personal growth.

A teachable mind is fundamental in obtaining both.

The zest to gain knowledge is a powerful gift.

It evokes confidence, credence, and it positively uplifts.

*A Journey Through Life's Moments*

# Reflections

# Disappointments

Surely as we live, we will experience setbacks that cause a major impact.

It is to be expected as a matter of fact.

No matter how much time and energy we give to plans and details.

Our dreams are subject to unpredictable and arbitrary **derails.**

Disappointments are plans that did not achieve the expected outcome.

Or sometimes a person who seems not to be who they were perceived to become.

Disappointments produce sadness, dissatisfaction, and even pain.

They are not easily disguised, the effort to try would certainly be in vain.

The result of being disappointed does not have to be negative.

Don't we believe that all matters produce something positive?

One of the most unfailing facts of life's experiences,

Is that a closer look reveals hidden or ignored variances.

When we take an up-close look at the full picture.
We see all the intricate parts of this mood-altering structure.
Then we have motive, reality, and practicality in a clear view.
We can honestly assess parts to omit and which to renew.

Disappointments are great motivators if we use them well.
They help us become thorough in our endeavors to excel.
Their unforgettable bite leaves a small but lasting scar.
Reminding us to pray, ponder, and pursue in order to go far.

# Reflections

# Willful Blindness

Unable to behold beauty in nature like water flowing in a quiet stream.
Robbed of the gift to view a brilliantly colored flower from the sun's highest beam.
Gazing into the face of a newborn child,
Marveling at God's handiwork, so precious and undefiled.

Physical blindness seems to be a harsh and unbearable condition.
Being deprived of the ability to explore, discover, or make an observation.
Some may think that it is so undeserved and unfair.
No one should have this heavy burden to bear.

I remember hearing a blind man say.
I am not blind; I can see in multiple ways.
I see with my sense of touch, hearing, and smell.
I am more than capable of describing something in extraordinary detail.

# Rhymes for Every Reason and Season

Willful blindness has self-made traits and tendencies.

This blindness's origin comes from one's own defenses and personal biases.

The desire not to see is a protective shield.

A weapon of war used on an emotional battlefield.

The willfully blind appear to be uncaring and unempathetic.

They show little concern for others' feelings – no matter how dramatic.

They offer the persona of always being in control.

On top of every situation and achieving the goal.

Most times things are in no way as they seem.

There is a little child carefully hidden behind the scenes.

If you look closely, she has tears in her eyes.

She dried them every time the shield was raised high.

She is not crying because she is afraid of a fight.

She has been in hard emotional battles all her life.

No, she is crying because no one displayed genuine love and affection for her,

when she was young and eager for an abundant life journey to occur.

*A Journey Through Life's Moments*

# Reflections

# 28

# GRIEF

An experience that leaves a void or sense of loss.
An emotional stain that cannot be removed or covered by a magical gloss.
The hurt it brings is strong and can penetrate even the deepest core.
It is too severe, too extreme, and too intense to ignore.

Grief is a combination of indescribable sorrow and unwelcome change.
It dictates the ability to engage in daily activities and it controls the scope and range.
Making it difficult to enjoy close relationships that once brought pure delight.
Reducing them to no more than a superficial encounter – just to be polite.

*A Journey Through Life's Moments*

Grief is an emotionally healing process that we cannot bypass or overlook.

No amount of self-discipline or mood-altering technique can compete with its magnetizing hook.

Grief must perform its duty, and it does not discriminate or show favor.

Grief goes with every experience of loss – without waver.

All components of grief play a vital role in the pursuit of inner peace.

They come and they go at will, with the authority to surge or simply cease.

They do not follow each other in a strict, clearly defined line.

Their appearance is random with an oddly-timed design.

Comfort can be found in the midst of such tremendous pain.

The passing of time allows healthy healing to be attained.

The memory of sorrow will never be fully erased.

But time causes fond memories to take its place.

# Reflections

# 29

# A Family

Wherever you find social commonality
There you will hear the phase "just like family."
People's view of family is quite complex
Their opinions are formed from upbringing, one may suspect.

Some believe a family is formed strictly by blood or adoption.
While others think there are many other options.
Some say a real family has children and two parents.
Another is sure a family can exist and flourish with one parent absent.

A family in the true meaning and application of the word.
Are individuals sharing common dialogue, to outsiders is unheard.
Family people know each other individually and collectively.
They respect diversity yet are united unequivocally.

# Rhymes for Every Reason and Season

All units referred to as family may not be family at all.
Any group filled with love and support may qualify for the call.
Who has the authority to say yea or nay.
Maybe it is, or maybe it's not- it's not for us to say.

*A Journey Through Life's Moments*

# Reflections

# 30

# Am I a Solider

If I honestly believe the Battle is the Lord's and not Mine
Then why do I carry my defensive weapons at all times?
My fiercest enemy is elusive and sometimes invisible, far too crafty for me to see.
So, my self-made weapons are inadequate to shield and protect me.

My foe also uses people close by, to catch me off- guard.
Because I'm not expecting them to attack and tear me apart.
Keeping my head on a swivel is the advice the world offers.
But the constant movement causes my creativity to become stagnant or falter.

At the point of despair, past victories are brought to my remembrance.
Thoughts of overcoming obstacles make their triumphant entrance.
My heart swells with joy and grateful praise.
Acknowledging God's faithfulness and his amazing grace.

I resolve that in life there will be tests and trials.

God permits them to come, and they may last for a while.

Through every challenge I faced, I first thought I would not overcome.

I now know, the Battle was God's all along and He has already won.

# Reflections

# 31

# Love and Victory

Love is an intense emotion that produces action.
Victory is the result of defeat that may or may not bring satisfaction.
Most people have experienced both along life's way.
They shape our thoughts and the things we say.

Love is a natural feeling that is necessary for a healthy existence.
There is no comparable substitute for its absence.
It provides balance and self-assurance.
That can withstand harsh emotional tests with equal resistance.

Trophies, accolades, and awards are reminders that we achieved success.
They temporarily bring a sense of fulfillment and happiness.
But if victory is not accompanied by love.
It fades like a cut flower or a balloon rising high above.

# Rhymes for Every Reason and Season

Love and victory together are an incredibly lasting pair.

They do not lose strength even though they are shared.

They enhance each other's power.

Victory is sweeter as love grows stronger.

*A Journey Through Life's Moments*

# Reflections

# 32

## The Message

I want my message to be loud and clear.
Leaving no room for misinterpretation or ill will.
My words and deeds agree with each other.
What I say and what I do- not sway or waiver.

Consistency and patience show in my everyday affairs.
Not yielding to being judgmental and unwilling to share.
I desire to be a defender of moral justice.
But equally promoting mercy as my instinctive practice.

I pray to have a seat at the Wisdom Table.
Equipped to impart useful counsel that is just and stable.
My record reflect what I said and what I exhibited is right.
I did not compromise for the sake of being polite.

My desired message comes from a place of deep humility.

I know I cannot achieve it with my own human ability.

God is the giver of this noble message.

I look to him to deliver this divine package.

# Reflections

# 33

# Where Did They Go

We say respect and reverence are rarely seen.
They are not clearly recognized in our daily routines.
People just do not display these honorable traits.
While dealing with others in small matters or great.

What happened to graciously greeting everyone we meet?
Whether someone well-known or a stranger on the street.
Men quickly giving a woman their seat.
Being a normal gesture-not so gallant or unique.

Perceiving, "Thank you" and "you're welcome" as ancient responses or ritual.
Especially remarkable if uttered by a young individual,
And showing respect for another's personal space
Being an odd practice to observe in a public place.

# Rhymes for Every Reason and Season

Who is responsible for preserving these traditions?
Who allowed respect and reverence to be put out of commission?
Have they been tucked away in a cluttered drawer?
With old things they don't plan to use anymore.

Maybe now is the opportune time.
To bring them to the frontline.
They have not lost their style or fragrances
They just need us to exhibit their value and relevance.

*A Journey Through Life's Moments*

# Reflections

# WHY?

You start a new task with vigor and great speed.
Only to lose interest or stop when a loved one disagrees.
Our goals and ambitions seem too hard, even unreachable.
No matter how much time is spent, the end appears not to be possible.

You believe if you live right, satisfaction and contentment is a foregone conclusion.
The efforts you involve yourself in produce only conflict and confusion.
Failure and incomplete projects clutter your mind to the point of despair.
You wonder what is your purpose and if life is truly fair.

Should we be asking the more important questions?
What is the reason for our negative self-perception?
Are we in tune with our unique gifts and abilities?
Or have we allowed social trends to limit our inner visibility?
We all possess meaningful talents that are unique to us.

We are designed to create, generate, or construct.
If we do not finish the work, we start.
Or if completed, it does not bring joy to the heart.
It is time to take an honest look inside.
Then find the decisive answer to the question, why?

# Reflections

# 35

## Who Are You

Does the temperature change when you enter a room?
Do people stop and look at you when you are passing through?
Do others pay attention to what you have to say?
Has someone acknowledged words you shared with them from another day?

Do you give cheerfully to those who are without?
Do you desire to be steadfast and utterly devout?
Does the condition of the world matter to you?
Do you pray for miracles to come true?

Does crime and mischief disturb your peace?
Are you shocked when justice is not achieved?
Are you willing to represent those who may be overlooked or forgotten?
Will you stand for the weak and the downtrodden?

# Rhymes for Every Reason and Season

If you care about others and dare to positively act
The sincerity of your cause will be evident, as a matter of fact.
Showing love and support wherever it is needed.
Is note-worthy and will be contagiously repeated.

*A Journey Through Life's Moments*

# Reflections

# Your Song

A song was placed in every human heart.
The words and tune ring out in life circumstances, with no regard.
Every verse and refrain come from deep within
Combining the tempo and beat for a harmonious blend.

I cannot sing yours and you cannot sing mine.
The tune was uniquely fashioned by God's design.
We were ordained to be different- one of a kind.
It is waste of valuable time to imitate what others were assigned.

It is our job to perfect our distinctive song.
The usage of words given to another would be undeniably wrong.
Staying true to what we were created to be.
Produces joy and contentment to the superlative degree.

*A Journey Through Life's Moments*

# Reflections

# 37

## Ordinary

How can we accurately describe a human being?
As of no distinction, nothing unique or amazing
Without any superior quality that sets them apart.
Only plain, simple, and common – no unusual traits of any sort.

Many are of the belief that people are just people, all of one kind.
Creatures of habit and behavior that are predictably unrefined.
In any given situation they respond similarly to a social controversy.
Never willing to stand alone for fear of isolation with no mercy.

But there appears to be a notable contradiction.
Were not individuals supposed to be made singular without duplication?
No two people, even twins, perform in automatic synchrony.
There are noticeable differences in their natural form, expressions, and agility.

Generalizations, stereotypes, and shallow assumptions

May account for this unreliable and debatable conclusion.

The meaning of ordinary must vary from one person to the next.

Perhaps the definition was culturally changed or taken out of context.

There is nothing normal or ordinary in relation to humanity.

Everyone is given a specific purpose and equipped with full capability.

Every part of every person crafted for an individualized mission.

A journey predestined long before their existence came to full fruition.

**Rhymes for Every Reason and Season**

# Reflections

# Confidence or Arrogance

Not allowing fear to overtake you.

Speaking the truth in the presence of the powerful – many or a few.

Making your position clear without compromise or waver.

Giving little consideration to the outcome or losing favor.

Confidence comes from a place of deep trust.

A firm belief in something or someone proven to be faithful and just.

It stands on unbendable rules.

The most dependable and lasting of all tools.

Arrogance is confidence and pride in total exaggeration.

It connects with rudeness, conceit, and high self-estimation.

Harboring thoughts of complete superiority.

Displaying impolite behavior and limitless audacity.

# Rhymes for Every Reason and Season

Confidence and arrogance are often compared.

Because both involve information being expressed and boldly shared.

But their source is what makes the difference.

Arrogance relies on itself but confidence depends on truth and temperance.

Confidence is a precious, treasured gift.

It is a possession that empowers and uplifts.

Confidence is acquired without compensation.

It is available to ALL with no discrimination.

*A Journey Through Life's Moments*

# Reflections

# 39

# Dim or Dazzle

At the end of each of our days
We usually rank it in two extremely distinct ways.
If we accomplished what we planned to do.
We deem it a good day – no unfinished issue.

But if our day involved stress, pain, or controversy.
We classify it as a bad day–filled with challenges and no mercy.
Feelings of defeat and even sadness.
Take full control leaving no room for calm or hopefulness.

Could or should a day be summed up in such a broad manner?
Could there be more to see if we looked a little deeper?
Could we get a better view if we stood at another angle?
Could the focus be changed or untangled?

*A Journey Through Life's Moments*

If we allow ourselves to take a broader view,

Giving meaningful thought to daily events – valuing every moment, not just a few!

Our labeling method may evolve greatly.

As we observe beauty and blessings that appear daily!

Yes, some days seem dimmed by a traumatic or tragic event.

While another day may seem to dazzle because of a dynamic, exciting announcement!

Both had some good outcomes and some bad incidents.

Our path gets brighter when we can make a daily eye-opening assessment.

When applying gratefulness, thankfulness, and optimism,

Our outlook on life takes on renewed enthusiasm.

We then see the priceless value of the sunshine and the rain.

And appreciate their rhythmic purpose and unfailing musical refrain.

**Rhymes for Every Reason and Season**

# Reflections

*A Journey Through Life's Moments*

# 40

# Miss Lollygag

Lady, you have matters that need your undivided attention.
What have you been doing that has caused this huge deviation?
According to your bold predictions of your lifestyle success
There should be, at least, signs of your forward progress.

You told us you would be a powerful force on the earth.
You would be world renowned and be of enormous worth.
Your beauty and talents would take you to the highest social heights.
You would never have to worry about the weightier matters of life.

I hear you say, just wait, my pause is only temporary.
But I say, please take the word "wait" from your vocabulary.
And replace it with these words: focus, discipline, start, and finish.
Then you will notice that procrastination will surely diminish.

# Rhymes for Every Reason and Season

Where is your written life plan?

Take it from the bottom of the stack and put it in your hand.

Review the details from the first step to the last.

Make the necessary modifications or simply recast.

Remember, time does not stop to make a friend.

It stays true to its course that never ends.

Time will not slow down for anyone to regroup.

It stays in step like a precision military troop.

Here are my words of encouragement to you.

Get up, stand up, and recommit to your course to persist and pursue.

All your dreams and hopes are still yet to be claimed.

Your forward steps will result in a successful EXCLAIM!

*A Journey Through Life's Moments*

# Reflections

**Rhymes for Every Reason and Season**

# Mr. Man

You are a magnificent specimen of divine craftsmanship.

Built to physically carry heavy loads with remarkable showmanship.

You display the strength of a mighty warrior.

Powerful enough to withstand any obstacle or barrier.

Your strong voice and broad steps capture our attention.

We believed you were in charge before your position was ever mentioned.

You appear confident and eager to complete.

Any project assigned to you-never entertaining a failure or defeat.

But before you left your place of abode.

You were in the mist of an emotional crisis – ready to explode.

You feared someone might uncover your deceptive mask.

The one you wear when you are forced to undertake a new task.

You were taught to play your proud manly role well.
Talk Tough, Be Strong and if you cry, never tell.
Bury your disappointments deep in the dirt.
So no one can find them and expose your hurt.

Sir, please let someone into your heart.
Your power will not dissolve or be torn apart.
Nourishing support will enhance your pursuit of lasting success.
Embrace it, cherish it, it will be your most meaningful conquest.

# Reflections

*A Journey Through Life's Moments*

# 42

# Something Precious

There are so many precious moments to be observed each day.

Hidden in clear view are priceless treasures on display.

Memorable acts of love and kindness can always be found.

If we would but look for them in ordinary situations that are all around.

Times spent with family and friends are some of those common occurrences.

We discount them as routine or traditions, not embracing their full substance.

Telling the old familiar stories at every family gathering

Create a strong bond of togetherness and a sense of belonging.

Hearing the genuine laughter of a child at play.

And listening to them explain why they did not obey.

# Rhymes for Every Reason and Season

These are precious memories that last a lifetime.
We are seeing developing character that they will later refine.

Precious things are not so rare.
They are just overshadowed by distractions of daily care.
Treasuring life's invaluable events are quite easy to do.
It takes open eyes, open minds, and hearts that seek joy in every color and hue.

*A Journey Through Life's Moments*

# Reflections

# 43

## Blame and Shame

A well-known notorious set of twins.

Who work closely together always expecting to win?

Do not look to them for comfort or support.

They are relentlessly brutal with no compassion to export.

This pair freely roams where sadness and defeat live.

Homesteading in the hearts of those who are overwhelmed by failure and fear.

They assume their position in the heart and soul.

Of those who are struggling to regain their balance and be made whole.

This couple is such a crafty and infamous team.

After Blame has assigned its faults and lowered self-esteem

Then Shame does its job to cause lasting humiliation and distress

Together their goal is to forcibly conquer and suppress.

*A Journey Through Life's Moments*

We must work diligently not to let them win.
Surely, we have some strength left to at least defend.
Parts of our shattered plans and unfulfilled dreams
All is never lost, there is always something for us to redeem.

**Rhymes for Every Reason and Season**

# Reflections

Made in the USA
Columbia, SC
02 March 2025